P9-DTJ-120

WINGS OF WAR

Airplanes of World War II

by Nancy Robinson Masters

Content Review:

Research Department

United States Air Force Museum

C A P S T O N E
H I G H / L O W B O O K S
an imprint of Capstone Press

C A P S T O N E   P R E S S

818 North Willow Street • Mankato, Minnesota 56001
http://www.capstone-press.com

Library of Congress Cataloging-in-Publication Data
Robinson Masters, Nancy.
   Airplanes of World War II/by Nancy Robinson Masters.
      p. cm.--(Wings of war)
   Includes bibliographical references and index.
   Summary: An introduction to the different kinds of airplanes used in World
War II, including information about airplane parts and pilots' codes.
ISBN 1-56065-531-3
   1. Airplanes, Military--United States--History--Juvenile literature.
2. World War, 1939-1945--Aerial operations, American--Juvenile literature.
[1. Airplanes, Military. 2. World War 1939-1945--Aerial operations.] I. Title.
II. Title: Airplanes of World War Two. III. Title: Airplanes of World War 2. IV.
Series: Wings of war (Mankato, Minn.)
UG1242.R63 1998
623.7'461'09044--DC21

                                   97-5996
                                     CIP
                                     AC

The author would like to thank Harry Wadsworth, Laura Thaxton, and Bill
Masters for their research assistance.

Editorial credits
Editor, Matt Doeden; cover design, Timothy Halldin; illustrations, James
   Franklin, Timothy Halldin; photo research, Michelle L. Norstad

Photo credits
American Airpower Heritage Museum, 12, 14, 20, 22, 29
Archive Photos, 4, 6, 9, 30
Steve Butman, 40
Nancy Robinson Masters, cover, 25
National Archives, 35, 36
Larry Sanders, 17, 18, 26, 38, 42

TABLE OF CONTENTS

CHAPTER ONE

Flying into World War II

Adolf Hitler used a powerful German air force to attack Poland in 1939. The attack started World War II (1939-1945).

The German military joined the Japanese and Italian militaries to form the Axis powers. The Axis powers fought against the Allied nations. The Allied nations included Canada, Great Britain, France, and Russia.

Germany used a powerful air force to attack Poland in 1939.

U.S. Entry

The United States did not enter World War II until 1941. In 1941, the Japanese military attacked Pearl Harbor, Hawaii with more than 300 airplanes. The Japanese forces bombed a U.S. Navy base there.

The attack on Pearl Harbor killed more than 2,000 people. It destroyed almost every U.S. ship at the base. The attack also destroyed hundreds of U.S. aircraft.

The United States joined the Allied nations after the attack. The United States built more than 100,000 new airplanes for World War II. The U.S. Army Air Forces used most of the airplanes. The U.S. Air Force was part of the Army during World War II. The U.S. Navy and Marines also used some of the airplanes. Other Allied nations used the rest of the airplanes.

The Japanese attack on Pearl Harbor destroyed almost every ship at the base.

Training for War

The United States did not wait until 1941 to prepare for World War II. The United States began preparing as soon as the war started in 1939. U.S. leaders knew they might need to enter the war. They also knew the United States would need a strong air force.

The U.S. military began training pilots, navigators, and bombardiers for war. Navigators map courses for pilots to fly. Bombardiers control where and when bombs drop from airplanes. The military also trained people to operate airplane guns and fix engines.

The military trained pilots to fly different kinds of aircraft. Most pilots learned to fly fighters, bombers, or transports.

War's End

World War II lasted until 1945. The Allied nations fought the Axis powers in Europe and above the Pacific Ocean. The two sides fought battles in the air, on the ground, and on the ocean.

The U.S. military trained pilots for World War II.

AFTERNOON WING

No 3 BOARD

In early 1945, the United States and Russia forced the German military to surrender. Surrender means to give up a fight or a battle. The war in Europe ended.

But the Japanese military kept fighting. The U.S. military fought the Japanese military on the Pacific Ocean. The Allies were winning the war. The U.S. military bombed important Japanese cities. But Japan would not surrender. U.S. leaders knew they needed a major victory to make the Japanese military surrender.

During World War II, U.S. scientists invented the atomic bomb. An atomic bomb is a powerful explosive that destroys large areas. An atomic bomb leaves behind harmful elements after it explodes. The U.S. military was ready to use the atomic bomb in 1945.

On August 6, 1945, the U.S. military dropped an atomic bomb on Hiroshima, Japan. The military dropped another atomic bomb on Nagasaki, Japan, three days later. World War II ended August 14, 1945.

MAJOR PACIFIC AIR BATTLES OF WORLD WAR II

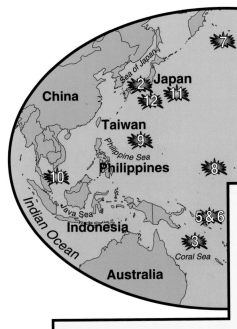

5. Guadalcanal Campaign,
    Aug., 1942 - Feb., 1943
6. Solomon Islands Campaign,
    Feb., 1943 - Nov.,1944
7. Battle of the Komandorski Islands,
    March 26, 1943
8. Truk Attack,
    Feb. 17-18, 1944
9. Battle of the Philippine Sea,
    June 19-20, 1944
10. Battle of Leyte Gulf,
    Oct. 23 - 26, 1944
11. Battle for Iwo Jima
    February, 1945
12. Atomic Bomb dropped on Hiroshima
    August 6, 1945

1. Pearl Harbor,
    Dec. 7,1941
2. Doolittle Raid
    April 18,1942
3. Battle of the Coral Sea,
    May 4-8, 1942
4. Battle of Midway,
    June 3-6, 1942

CHAPTER TWO

World War II Airplanes

The Allied nations needed many kinds of airplanes to win World War II. The military used different kinds of planes for different purposes during World War II. Fighters, bombers, transports, and trainers were the main kinds of airplanes. Manufacturers built each kind of airplane for a certain purpose.

Bombers had different purposes than fighters and transports.

World War II fighters were small and fast.

Fighters

World War II fighters were small and fast.
They could climb and turn quickly. They had
guns and cannons. Some carried bombs and
explosive rockets.

Fighters had several jobs during World War
II. Fighters were escorts for heavy bombers.
An escort is a fighter that flies with another

airplane to protect it. Fighter escorts flew above, below, and beside bombers to protect them from enemies.

Some fighters flew reconnaissance missions. A reconnaissance mission is a flight for gathering information about an enemy. Fighter pilots used special cameras to take pictures of enemies. The pictures helped bomber pilots know where important enemy bases were located.

Bombers

World War II bombers carried and dropped bombs. Bombers were large and heavy. But they could fly far and high.

The Allied nations had four main kinds of bombers. They were light, medium, heavy, and very heavy bombers. The largest World War II bomber was the Boeing B-29 Superfortress. The B-29 Superfortress was a very heavy bomber. One B-29 called the *Enola Gay* dropped the first atomic bomb on Japan.

Both the Axis powers and the Allied nations used dive bombers. Dive bombers spotted targets from as high as 12,000 feet (3,600 meters). A target is the object at which pilots aim their bombs. Dive bomber pilots dove to about 2,000 feet (about 600 meters) and released their bombs. The Allies used the Dauntless SBD as a dive bomber. The German air force used the German Junkers Ju-87 Stuka.

Transports

World War II transports carried supplies to people in combat areas. Combat is fighting between militaries. Some transports carried airplane gasoline. The Allies needed large amounts of gasoline for each bombing mission. One group of heavy bombers could use more than 16,000 gallons (60,800 liters) of gasoline on a mission. Transports supplied most of this gasoline.

World War II transports carried supplies to people in combat areas.

Pilots learned to fly in small airplanes called trainers.

Transports also carried food and medical supplies. Some transports moved soldiers from base to base. Others carried prisoners or wounded soldiers.

Trainers

Most people who became World War II pilots began with no experience flying airplanes. They started by flying airplanes called trainers.

The Allied nations trained pilots to fly each kind of airplane. Pilots started by learning to fly airplanes in small trainers like the Stearman Kaydet. These were tandem airplanes. Tandem means having two seats, one behind the other. Instructors flew with the new pilots in these airplanes.

Pilots learned to fly big trainers after they could fly small trainers. American pilots trained with the North American AT-6 Texan. Most bomber pilots then trained with the Beech AT-11 Kansan. Most transport pilots trained with the AT-10 and AT-17.

The Axis powers trained most of their pilots before World War II. Many Japanese pilots learned to fly during a war against China in the 1930s. Many German pilots learned to fly during the Spanish Civil War in the late 1930s.

CHAPTER THREE

Parts of World War II Airplanes

Manufacturers built many new airplanes during World War II. Each kind of airplane had its own purpose. Manufacturers built each kind differently.

But most of the airplanes had the same basic parts. They had airframes, wings, propellers, and landing gear.

Most World War II airplanes had airframes, wings, propellers, and landing gear.

Airframes

The airframe is the main part of an aircraft. An airframe includes the fuselage and the wings. The fuselage is the long body of the plane that carries the cargo and crew. Cargo is the supplies carried by an aircraft.

Most World War II airplanes had metal airframes. Manufacturers used aluminum to build airframes. Some smaller planes like trainers had wooden airframes. Others had airframes made of steel.

Wings

Wings connect to the sides of the fuselage. Wings are also called airfoils. The airfoils on most World War II airplanes were metal. Some were wood. Light metal or cloth covered the wings and the fuselage.

The size and shape of wings affect how airplanes fly. They affect how high and how

Wings are also called airfoils.

fast airplanes can travel. They also affect how quickly airplanes can turn.

Engines

Engines produce the power that moves airplanes through the air. Airplanes had two types of engines during World War II. They had in-line engines and radial engines. An in-line engine had all of its cylinders in a straight row. Some in-line engines had cylinders arranged in the shape of a V. A radial engine had its cylinders arranged in a circle. A cylinder is a tube-shaped part of an engine that fills with gas and air. An engine's power is produced in the cylinders.

Large airplanes like heavy bombers had very powerful engines. Some large airplanes had more than one engine.

Fighters and trainers usually had smaller engines. The smaller engines did not produce as much power.

Engines produce the power that moves airplanes through the air.

Propellers

A propeller is a set of blades on the front of an airplane. A propeller moves through the air like a fan. It pushes the air back over and under the airplane's wings. This keeps the airplane flying.

Some World War II airplanes had variable-pitch propellers. Pitch is the angle of propeller blades. A variable-pitch propeller changes the flow of air over the wings. When the air flow changes, the airplane's speed changes.

Some modern airplanes have variable-pitch propellers. Many modern airplanes have engines so powerful that they do not need propellers. These airplanes are called jets.

Landing Gear

Landing gear is an airplane's wheels. Most World War II combat airplanes had

A propeller moves through the air like a fan.

retractable landing gear. Retractable landing gear folds into the wings or the fuselage of an airplane. Retractable landing gear allows an airplane to climb quickly and fly fast.

Some World War II airplanes had fixed landing gear. Fixed landing gear stayed down all the time. The airplanes with fixed landing gear flew slower than those with retractable landing gear.

Dive Flaps

Some World War II airplanes had dive flaps on their wings. Dive flaps allowed pilots to make steep dives. Dive flaps kept dive bombers from dropping too fast. Dive bombers that dropped too fast would break apart in the air.

The Douglas SBD Dauntless was one Allied airplane with dive flaps. The Dauntless was a bomber the U.S. Navy used over the Pacific Ocean. German Ju-87 Stukas also had dive flaps.

World War II airplanes had either fixed or retractable landing gear.

CHAPTER FOUR

Airplane Codes

Pilots often used codes to speak to one another. They used some secret codes to keep enemies from understanding messages. Other codes were easy to understand. They were not secret codes.

Alphabet Code

World War II pilots used an alphabet code to communicate. It was often difficult for pilots to understand each other on airplane radios. Pilots used the alphabet code when they had to spell

U.S. pilots often used codes to speak to one another.

Pilots used a special list of code words in World War II.
Each word represented a letter. Pilots could understand
one another better by using this list.

A ble	**N** an
B aker	**O** boe
C harlie	**P** eter
D og	**Q** ueen
E asy	**R** oger
F ox	**S** ugar
G eorge	**T** are
H ow	**U** ncle
I tem	**V** ictor
J ig	**W** illiam
K ing	**X** ray
L ove	**Y** oke
M ike	**Z** ebra

A pilot who wanted to say seven might say:
Sugar Easy Victor Easy Nan.

important words. Pilots used words to represent letters so they would always understand each other. Pilots used the word Able to represent the letter A. They used Zebra to represent Z. Every letter had a code word.

Pilots still use the alphabet code today. But some of the words have changed. Queen represented the letter Q during World War II. Now pilots use Quebec to represent Q.

Aircraft Labels

Pilots used code letters to label airplanes during World War II. Letters also identified the kinds of missions airplanes flew.

Some airplanes like the B-29 used the letter B for identification. The B stood for bomber. Transports like the C-47 used the letter C. The C stood for cargo. Some airplanes like the A-26 used the letter A. The A stood for attack.

Before World War II, pilots called fighters pursuit airplanes. Pursuit airplanes like the P-

51 used the letter P for identification. Even after pursuit airplanes became known as fighters, they used the letter P for identification.

X, Y, and Z

The U.S. military also used letters to identify the development of World War II airplanes. An airplane had an X before its name while the military built it. For example, the P-38 Lightning was the XP-38 while the military manufactured it.

An airplane had a Y before its name if the military was testing it. The XP-38 became the YP-38 when the military tested the first models. It became the P-38 when the tests were complete and the airplane was ready for combat.

The military used the letter Z with airplanes that had become obsolete. Obsolete means no longer useful. Many airplanes used when World War II began were obsolete when the war ended.

The military used letters to identify the development of World War II airplanes.

CHAPTER FIVE

Airplanes After the War

The U.S. military had many surplus airplanes after World War II. Surplus means more than is needed. The military sent some surplus airplanes to airplane graveyards. An airplane graveyard is a place where old or unneeded airplanes are kept. A few World War II airplanes remained in service. The military used them until they became obsolete.

The military sent some surplus airplanes to airplane graveyards.

Some World War II airplanes including the P-51 flew during the Korean War.

Action After the War

Some World War II airplanes flew in the
Korean War (1950-1953). The U.S. military
used the B-29 Superfortress, the AT-6 Texan,

and the P-51 Mustang during the Korean War. The P-51 was still one of the world's best fighter airplanes during the Korean War. The U.S. Navy used F4U Corsairs.

Surplus Airplanes

The U.S. military sold some surplus airplanes to the air forces of other countries. It used other surplus airplanes to carry supplies. The military took most World War II airplanes apart and melted them in smelters. A smelter is a furnace where metal is melted.

Manufacturers reused metal from the airplanes to make window screens and other items for construction. The United States sent many of these items to Germany, Italy, and Japan. The metal helped these countries rebuild after World War II.

World War II Airplanes Today

Some World War II airplanes are in museums. They cannot fly anymore. The National Museum of Naval Aviation has more than 150 airplanes. Many of them are from World War II.

The National Air and Space Museum in Washington, D.C., displays parts of the *Enola Gay*. The museum does not display the whole plane because it is too large. It displays the *Enola Gay's* cockpit, engines, and bomb bay.

A few World War II airplanes are still flying. Museums and collectors buy the old airplanes and restore them. Restore means to bring an object back to its original condition.

Collectors often display airplanes at air shows. Some display their airplanes so visitors can see and touch them. Some fly their airplanes in front of crowds. Others

Some collectors fly World War II airplanes at air shows.

sell rides in their airplanes. World War II
airplanes like the AT-6 Texan and the P-51
Mustang are popular at air shows.

tail

gun turret

fuselage

Grumman TBM bomber

wing

cockpit

nose

propeller

WORDS TO KNOW

bombardier (bom-buh-DIHR)—a bombing crew member who controls where and when bombs drop from airplanes

cargo (KAR-goh)—the supplies carried by an aircraft

cylinder (SIL-uhn-dur)—a tube-shaped part of an engine that fills with gas and air

escort (ESS-kort)—a fighter that protects a bomber

fuselage (FYOO-suh-lahzh)—the long body of an airplane that carries the cargo and crew

navigator (NAV-uh-gay-tuhr)—a bombing crew member who maps a course for the pilot to fly

obsolete (ob-suh-LEET)—no longer useful

propeller (pruh-PEL-ur)—a set of blades on the front of an airplane

reconnaissance (ree-KON-uh-suhnss)—a flight to gather information about an enemy

surplus (SUR-pluhss)—more than is needed

surrender (suh-REN-dur)—to give up a fight or battle

tandem (TAN-duhm)—having two seats, one in front of the other

TO LEARN MORE

Baines, Francesca. *Planes*. New York: Franklin Watts, 1995.

Masters, Nancy Robinson. *Bombers of World War II*. Mankato, Minnesota: Capstone High/Low Books, 1998.

Masters, Nancy Robinson. *Fighter Planes of World War II*. Mankato, Minnesota: Capstone High/Low Books, 1998.

Schleifer, Jay. *Bomber Planes*. Minneapolis: Capstone Press, 1996.

USEFUL ADDRESSES

National Air and Space Museum
Seventh Street and Independence Avenue
Washington, DC 20560

National Aviation Museum
P.O. Box 9724
Ottawa, Ontario KIG 543
Canada

Pima Air Museum
P.O. Box 17298
Tuscon, AZ 85731

Unites States Air Force Museum
Wright-Patterson Air Force Base
Dayton, OH 45433

INTERNET SITES

Enola Gay
http://www.nasm.edu/GALLERIES/GAL103/
   gal103.html

Welcome to the National Warplane Museum
http://www.warplane.org/

United States Air Force Museum
http://www.wpafb.af.mil/museum/

WWII Airplanes
http://canopus.lpi.msk.su/~watson/wwiiap.html

INDEX